CYGNUS THE SWAN

The Myth and Science of Astronomy

Simon Rose

openlightbox.com

LIGHTBOX

Go to **www.openlightbox.com**, and enter this book's unique code.

ACCESS CODE

LBB92892

Lightbox is an all-inclusive digital solution for the teaching and learning of curriculum topics in an original, groundbreaking way. Lightbox is based on National Curriculum Standards.

STANDARD FEATURES OF LIGHTBOX

AUDIO High-quality narration using text-to-speech system

ACTIVITIES Printable PDFs that can be emailed and graded

SLIDESHOWS Pictorial overviews of key concepts

VIDEOS Embedded high-definition video clips

WEBLINKS Curated links to external, child-safe resources

TRANSPARENCIES Step-by-step layering of maps, diagrams, charts, and timelines

INTERACTIVE MAPS Interactive maps and aerial satellite imagery

QUIZZES Ten multiple choice questions that are automatically graded and emailed for teacher assessment

KEY WORDS Matching key concepts to their definitions

Copyright © 2016 Smartbook Media Inc. All rights reserved.

Cygnus the Swan

Contents

Lightbox Access Code 2

Studying the Night Sky 4

Storytelling 6

Cygnus the Swan 8

The Origins of Cygnus 10

Astronomy through History 12

Cygnus over Time 14

Mapping Planetariums 16

Careers in Astronomy 18

Sky Facts 19

Astronomy Q and A 20

Make a Family Constellation 21

Know Your Stars Quiz 22

Key Words/Index 23

Log on to www.openlightbox.com 24

The Myth and Science of Astronomy

Studying the Night Sky

The study of stars and other objects in space is called astronomy. Groups of stars that form patterns in the night sky are known as constellations. They appear in different parts of the sky at different times of year. There are also some constellations that can be seen only from the Northern or the Southern **Hemisphere**. A star chart, or map of the sky, helps sky watchers find constellations.

Civilizations in the Middle East began naming stars and constellations thousands of years ago. About the same time, people named the signs of the zodiac. The zodiac is an imaginary band in the sky divided into 12 constellations that represent characters and animals. The first **telescopes** were used to study the stars in the early 17th century. Today, scientists called astronomers use large, powerful telescopes to observe **comets**, **galaxies**, stars, and planets. Planets are large objects in space that travel around a star, such as Earth or Mars moving around the Sun.

The signs of the zodiac appear in Turkish star maps from the 16th century.

A star is a huge glowing ball of very hot gas.

4   *Cygnus the Swan*

The largest constellation is Hydra. It covers more than 3 percent of the sky. *Hydra* means "water snake" in Latin. That was the language spoken in ancient Rome.

The brightest star in a constellation often has alpha as part of its scientific name. Alpha is the first letter of the Greek alphabet: α

The Myth and Science of Astronomy

Storytelling

Around the world, constellations have become part of folklore, or traditional customs, stories, and art. Throughout history, people have tried to explain the patterns they saw in the night sky. They created imaginary figures using the stars in the sky, as in a game of connect the dots. Some constellations were named after characters in ancient legends. Other constellations were named after animals. People also created stories about the figures in the night sky.

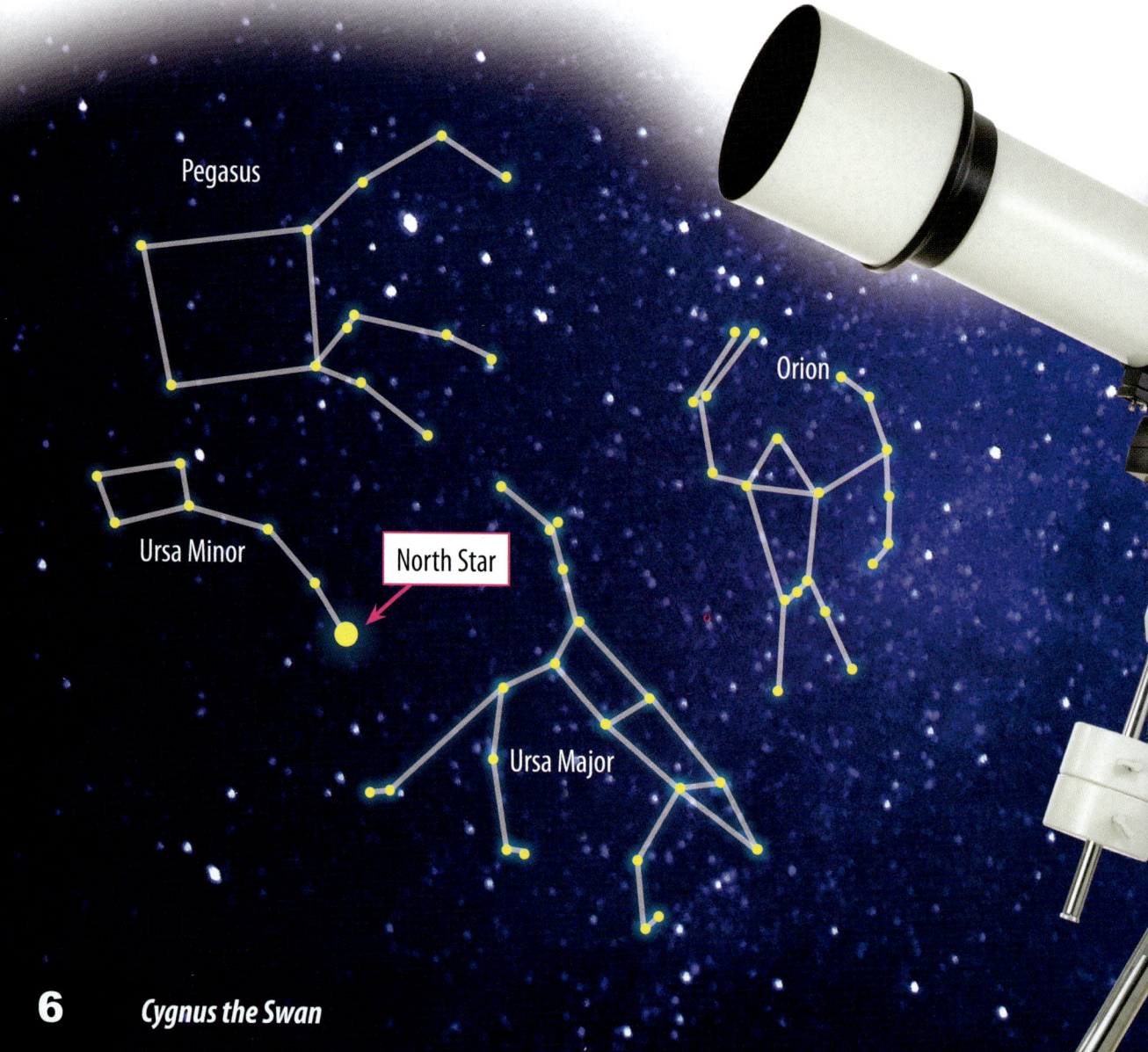

Cygnus the Swan

Some of the best-known constellations are seen in the Northern Hemisphere. They include Hercules, Pegasus, Ursa Major, Andromeda, Orion, and Cygnus. The Cygnus constellation is shown as a long-necked swan with its wings open.

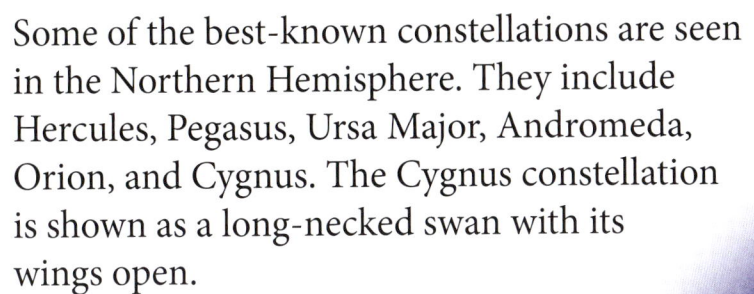

The Myth and Science of Astronomy

Cygnus the Swan

Many constellations are named after heroes. The heroes appear in stories about **supernatural** creatures and events. A collection of these stories is called mythology.

Who Was Cygnus?

The word *cygnus* means "swan" in Latin. After Rome took control of ancient Greece in the 100s BC, the Romans adopted many Greek gods and stories. Some of these stories included a swan or a character named Cygnus, which was also spelled Cycnus. In one story, Cycnus was the son of Ares, the god of war. Cycnus challenged a strong hero named Heracles, or Hercules, to a duel, and Cycnus died. Another story features Cycnus as the son of Poseidon, the god of the sea. This Cycnus fought in the Trojan War, a conflict between the Greeks and the people of the city of Troy. He was killed by the hero Achilles. In both stories, the Cycnus characters were changed into swans after dying.

The Cygnus constellation is linked to the Greek hero Orpheus. He was changed into a swan and put in the sky with his lyre, or stringed instrument, shown as the constellation Lyra.

The Story of Cygnus

A different Greek myth is about Cycnus and his friend Phaethon, the son of the Sun god. One day, the two friends were racing across the sky in carriages called chariots that were pulled by horses. However, when the friends traveled too close to the Sun, their chariots burned, and they both fell. When Cycnus awoke, Phaethon was trapped at the bottom of the Eridanus River. Cycnus could not reach his friend. Cycnus asked Zeus, the ruler of the gods, to change him into a swan. He agreed that he would live only as long as a swan. Zeus granted the request. As a swan, Cycnus was able to recover his friend's body for burial. Zeus was impressed by the sacrifice that Cycnus made. He placed an image of Cygnus in the night sky for all to see.

Italian artist Sebastiano Ricci painted *The Fall of Phaethon* in about 1703.

The Myth and Science of Astronomy

The Origins of Cygnus

The Greeks called the Cygnus constellation *Ornis*, which means "bird" in Greek. Arab astronomers described the star pattern as a hen. In China, the constellation tells the myth of a bridge formed by long-tailed birds called magpies. A farmer named Niu Lang and Zhi Nu, a fairy, wanted to marry. However, as a fairy, Zhi Nu was not allowed to marry a human. To keep the couple apart, the goddess of Heaven made a river in the sky, represented by the **Milky Way**. Once a year, according to the myth, all the magpies in the world join together to make a bridge over the river so the couple can be together. In the night sky, the Cygnus constellation serves as the bridge.

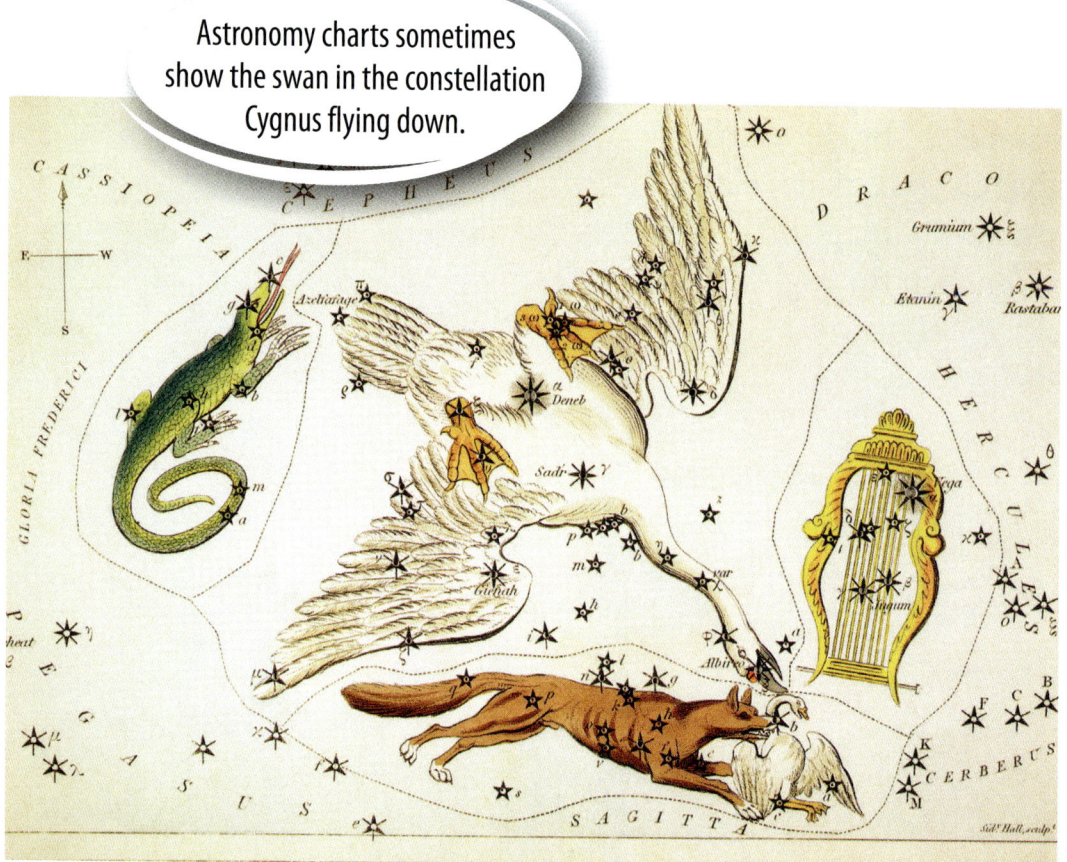

Astronomy charts sometimes show the swan in the constellation Cygnus flying down.

The Stars of Cygnus

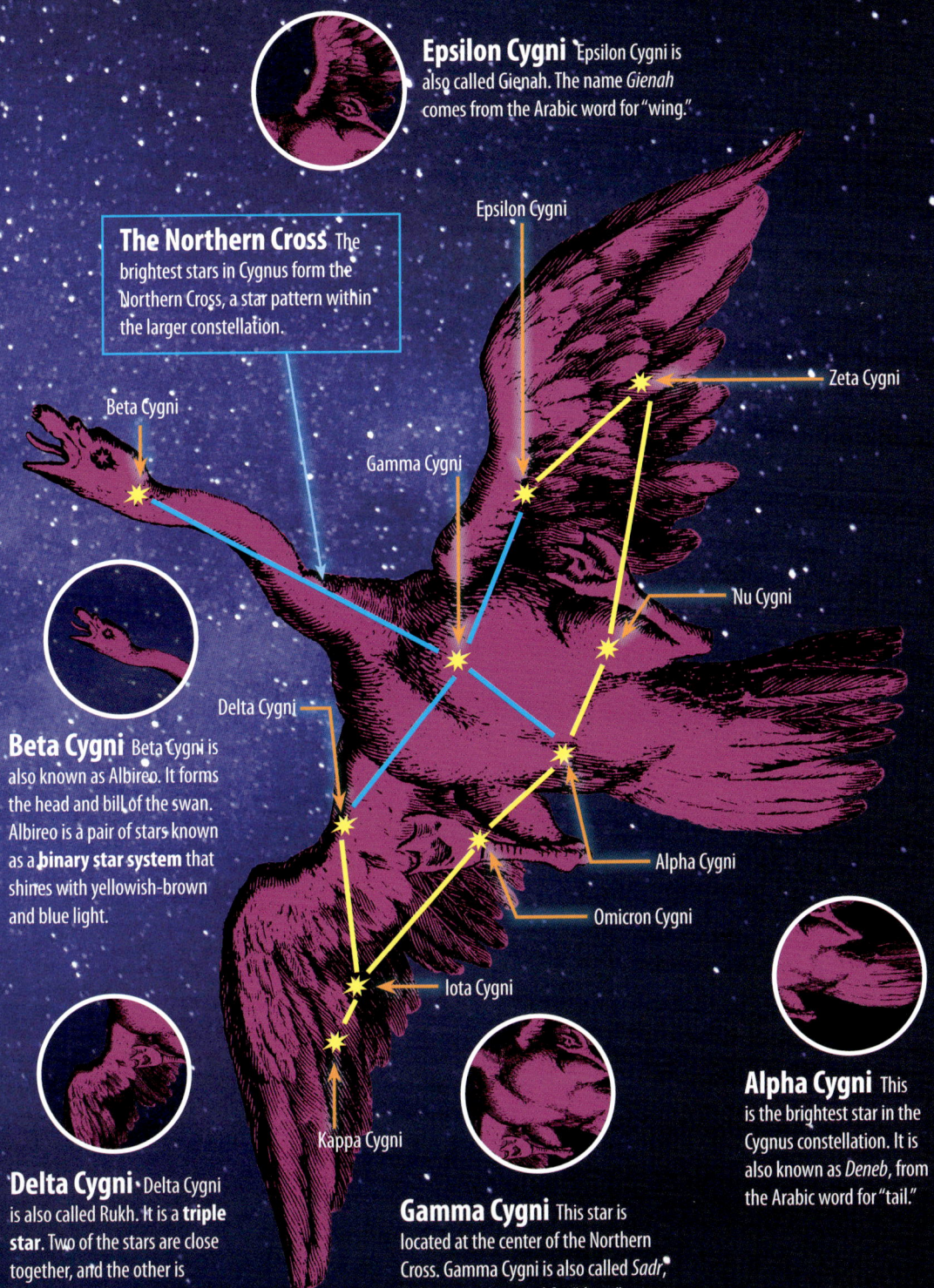

Epsilon Cygni Epsilon Cygni is also called Gienah. The name *Gienah* comes from the Arabic word for "wing."

The Northern Cross The brightest stars in Cygnus form the Northern Cross, a star pattern within the larger constellation.

Beta Cygni Beta Cygni is also known as Albireo. It forms the head and bill of the swan. Albireo is a pair of stars known as a **binary star system** that shines with yellowish-brown and blue light.

Delta Cygni Delta Cygni is also called Rukh. It is a **triple star**. Two of the stars are close together, and the other is farther away.

Gamma Cygni This star is located at the center of the Northern Cross. Gamma Cygni is also called *Sadr*, from the Arabic word for "chest."

Alpha Cygni This is the brightest star in the Cygnus constellation. It is also known as *Deneb*, from the Arabic word for "tail."

The Myth and Science of Astronomy

Astronomy through History

Map Based on Ptolemy's Research

AD 150

Akkadian Tablet

2500 BC
In Mesopotamia, the Akkadian civilization compiles the earliest known astronomy records.

130 BC
The Greek astronomer Hipparchus uses various tools to study the positions of stars. He creates the first accurate star map of more than 850 of the brightest stars.

350 BC
The Chinese astronomer Shi Shen creates a catalog of 800 stars.

3000 BC
The Sumerians, in the Middle East region known as Mesopotamia, make lists of the brightest stars and name the constellations in the zodiac for the first time.

Hipparchus

12 *Cygnus the Swan*

Johannes Kepler

1609
German astronomer Johannes Kepler publishes his laws about the motion of the planets. This is the first mathematical explanation that Earth revolves around the Sun.

1922
The International Astronomical Union names 88 official constellations. Of these, 36 constellations are in the northern sky, and 52 are in the southern sky.

1834
William Herschel's map of the sky defines the size and shape of the Milky Way, where Earth is located.

William Herschel

1990
The Hubble Space Telescope is launched.

Hubble Telescope

2018
The James Webb Space Telescope is scheduled for launch. More powerful than Hubble, it will search for galaxies not yet seen by humans.

The Myth and Science of Astronomy

Cygnus over Time

Astronomers have studied the Cygnus constellation for centuries. This group of stars appears in star charts in many ancient cultures around the world. In recent times, there have been some important scientific discoveries related to the Cygnus constellation.

1786 The North America Nebula in Cygnus

A **nebula** shaped like North America is located close to Deneb. It is a large red nebula. However, it is difficult to see without a telescope. William Herschel of Great Britain discovered the nebula in 1786.

1798 The Fireworks Galaxy in Cygnus

Herschel discovered the Fireworks Galaxy in 1798. It is a **spiral galaxy** between the Cygnus and Cepheus constellations. Astronomers have seen more **supernovas** in the Fireworks Galaxy than in any other.

1874 The Kappa Cygnids Meteor Shower

Hungarian astronomer Nicholas de Konkoly first saw the Kappa Cygnids **meteor** shower in 1874. A meteor shower is a large number of meteors that appear in the same area of the sky. Konkoly was observing the much-larger Perseid meteor shower when he noticed meteors near the star Kappa Cygni in Cygnus.

Cygnus the Swan

1904 Pickering's Triangle in Cygnus

Pickering's Triangle is part of the Veil Nebula in the Cygnus constellation. In 1904, U.S. astronomer Williamina Fleming discovered the triangle-shaped streaks of light, which are 1,500 **light-years** from Earth. Both Pickering's Triangle and the rest of the Veil Nebula were created by a supernova about 7,500 years ago.

2008 Cygnus and the Soap Bubble Nebula

David Jurasevich of the Mount Wilson **Observatory** in California discovered the Soap Bubble Nebula in the Cygnus constellation on July 6, 2008. The nebula is almost a perfect sphere, or the shape of a ball. It appears to float like a huge soap bubble, and astronomers are able to see through it.

2011 Kepler-22b in the Cygnus Constellation

The Kepler Space Telescope searches for planets that **orbit** other stars, not the Sun. It was launched in 2009. In 2011, it discovered the planet Kepler-22b in the Cygnus constellation. This was the first planet ever discovered that scientists believe might be able to support human life.

The Myth and Science of Astronomy

Mapping Planetariums

At a planetarium, visitors can see exhibits about space and images of the night sky. A large room in the planetarium, often called a sky theater, has a dome-shaped ceiling. Pictures of objects in space are shown on the ceiling, while viewers listen to information about those objects. Some planetariums have telescopes for visitors to see the night sky for themselves. This map shows where some of the best-known planetariums in the United States can be found.

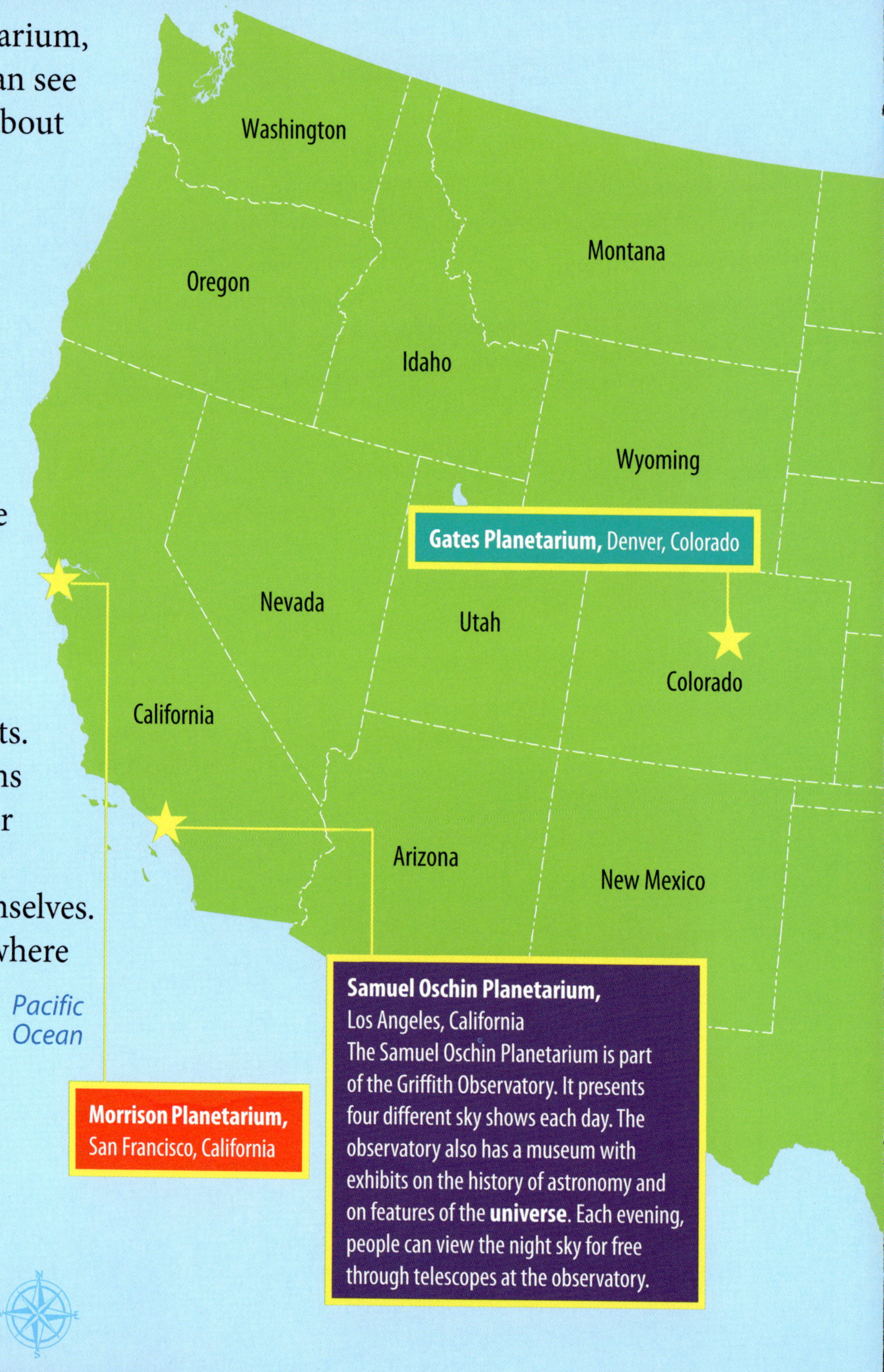

Gates Planetarium, Denver, Colorado

Morrison Planetarium, San Francisco, California

Samuel Oschin Planetarium, Los Angeles, California
The Samuel Oschin Planetarium is part of the Griffith Observatory. It presents four different sky shows each day. The observatory also has a museum with exhibits on the history of astronomy and on features of the **universe**. Each evening, people can view the night sky for free through telescopes at the observatory.

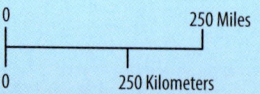

16   *Cygnus the Swan*

Adler Planetarium, Chicago, Illinois
The Adler Planetarium is a leader in science education. The planetarium has theater programs, exhibits featuring historic telescopes, and special events. In the Grainger Sky Theater, visitors learn about the night sky as they seem to journey through space.

Hayden Planetarium, New York, New York
The Hayden Planetarium is part of the Rose Center for Earth and Space at the American Museum of Natural History. The Hayden Sphere, which measures 87 feet (27 meters) across, houses the Space Theater in its top half. During many shows, visitors feel as if they are traveling through space.

Strasenburgh Planetarium, Rochester, New York

Albert Einstein Planetarium, Washington, D.C.

Morehead Planetarium, Chapel Hill, North Carolina

Burke Baker Planetarium, Houston, Texas

The Myth and Science of Astronomy

Careers in Astronomy

ASTRONOMERS often study for many years to prepare for their careers. Many future astronomers take classes in mathematics, physics, and other types of science during high school. At college, they often study physics, mathematics, engineering, and computer science. After graduating, many astronomers go on to receive a master's or doctor's degree. Astronomers often spend many years doing research to try to answer questions about objects in space.

TELESCOPE OPERATORS are the people who run and maintain large telescopes and related computer equipment. This job usually requires education in science, as well as technical and problem-solving skills. Telescope operators often work at night. They are responsible for running very expensive equipment.

COMPUTER SCIENTISTS design computer systems and hardware for scientific equipment. They may also program computers and develop software that astronomers and other scientists need in their work. People who want to be computer scientists often study physics, math, software engineering, and programming. Computer scientists need to be organized and have good problem-solving skills.

Cygnus the Swan

Sky Facts

A Witch's Broomstick

A bright cloud of gas and dust in the Veil Nebula looks like a witch's broomstick.

NOT SO LARGE

Earth's Sun appears bigger than other stars because it is closer to Earth. In fact, the Sun is only average in size. There are many stars that are much larger than Earth's Sun.

Sun

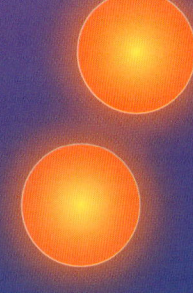

Closest to Home

The nearest star to Earth's Sun in the Cygnus constellation is a binary star system called 61 Cygni. However, it is still 11 light-years away. That is 65 trillion miles (105 trillion kilometers).

The Myth and Science of Astronomy

Astronomy Q and A

1 **Will humans ever travel to the stars?**
Not counting the Sun, the star nearest Earth is about 25.3 trillion miles (40.7 trillion km) away. At the speeds today's spacecraft can travel, it would take thousands of years to reach that star. Journeys to the stars may be possible in the future, but today, humans do not have the technology.

2 **Why do stars twinkle?**
Stars only seem to twinkle when seen from Earth. This is because of the effects of Earth's **atmosphere**. When light from stars enters the atmosphere, winds and areas with different temperatures affect it before the light reaches people's eyes. This causes the starlight to appear to twinkle.

3 **What is the largest star ever discovered?**
NML Cygni in the Cygnus constellation is the largest star ever discovered by astronomers. It is 1,650 times larger than the Sun. More than one billion Earths could fit inside NML Cygni.

4 **How many solar systems are in the universe?**
A solar system is a star and the planets orbiting it. Some stars besides the Sun are known to have planets, but scientists do not know how many. There are hundreds of billions of stars in the universe. Even if only a small portion have planets, there could still be billions of solar systems.

5 **Are all stars the same color?**
Stars come in a number of different colors. There are red, brown, orange, yellow, white, and blue stars. A star's color depends on how hot the star is. The coolest stars are red, and the hottest ones are blue.

Cygnus the Swan

Make a Family Constellation

Using bright stars visible in your area, you can create a new constellation about a member of your family or even a family pet. Give your star pattern a name. Then, you can make up a short story about the person or animal in your constellation.

What You Need:  Notebook — Pencil

1 Ask a parent for permission to go outside at night. Look for a clear section of the sky.

2 Find the brightest stars in that part of the night sky.

3 Draw the positions of these bright stars in your notebook. Be sure to have at least 10 different stars.

4 Connect the stars with lines to form a pattern, creating your own constellation. Who in your family does your pattern look like? What is the constellation called?

5 Create a story about your constellation. You can tell a made-up or true story based on your family member.

The Myth and Science of Astronomy

21

Know Your Stars Quiz

1. When was the Kepler Space Telescope launched?

2. What is the name of the brightest star in the Cygnus constellation?

3. In what city is the Hayden Planetarium?

4. What is the largest star ever discovered by astronomers?

5. What was the first planet ever discovered that might be able to support human life?

6. Who did Cycnus race across the sky in one Greek myth?

7. Which meteor shower was first spotted in the Cygnus constellation in 1874?

8. What year did William Herschel discover the North American Nebula?

9. What is Beta Cygni also known as?

10. What letter of the Greek alphabet often describes a constellation's brightest star?

ANSWERS: 1. 2009 2. Alpha Cygni 3. New York City 4. NML Cygni 5. Kepler-22b 6. Phaethon 7. The Kappa Cygnids 8. 1786 9. Albireo 10. Alpha

22 *Cygnus the Swan*

Key Words

atmosphere: the layer of air that surrounds Earth

binary star system: two stars that orbit a common center of gravity, the force that pulls objects toward one another

civilizations: groups of people who live in the same area and share beliefs and a way of life

comets: large balls of ice and rock in space that travel around the Sun

galaxies: groups of millions or billions of stars, as well as the dust and gas around them

hemisphere: one half of a sphere such as Earth

light-years: distances that light travels in one year

meteor: a piece of rock traveling in space that enters Earth's atmosphere, the layer of air around the planet

Milky Way: the galaxy that includes Earth and its solar system and appears as a white band of stars in the night sky

nebula: a large cloud of dust and gases in space

observatory: a building containing equipment used to observe and study stars, planets, weather, and other natural occurrences

orbit: to travel around an object in a curved path

spiral galaxy: a galaxy that has long arms curving around the center

supernatural: related to gods, spirits, or events that cannot be explained by science

supernovas: very large explosions that occur when huge stars die, or burn out

telescopes: devices used to detect and observe distant objects

triple star: a system of three stars that are held close to one another by gravity

universe: all of space and the objects in space

Index

Albireo 11, 22

Deneb 11, 14

Fireworks Galaxy 14
Fleming, Williamina 15

Hayden Planetarium 17, 22
Herschel, William 13, 14, 22

Hubble Space Telescope 13

Kappa Cygnids 14, 22
Kepler-22b 15, 22
Kepler, Johannes 13
Kepler Space Telescope 15, 22

NML Cygni 20, 22
North America Nebula 14, 22

Northern Cross 11

Rukh 11

Soap Bubble Nebula 15

Veil Nebula 15, 19

Zeus 9

The Myth and Science of Astronomy

LIGHTB◆X

➕ SUPPLEMENTARY RESOURCES

Click on the plus icon ➕ found in the bottom left corner of each spread to open additional teacher resources.

- Download and print the book's quizzes and activities
- Access curriculum correlations
- Explore additional web applications that enhance the Lightbox experience

LIGHTBOX DIGITAL TITLES
Packed full of integrated media

VIDEOS

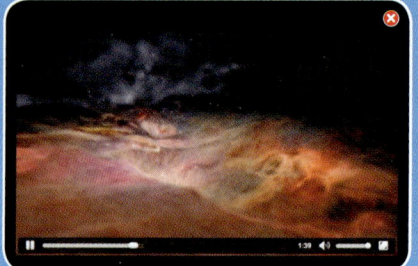

INTERACTIVE MAPS

WEBLINKS

SLIDESHOWS

QUIZZES

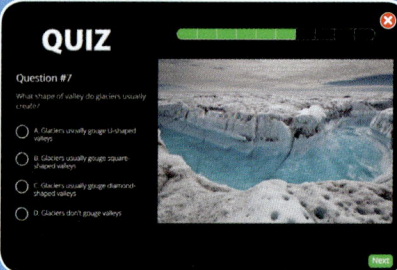

OPTIMIZED FOR
- ✓ TABLETS
- ✓ WHITEBOARDS
- ✓ COMPUTERS
- ✓ AND MUCH MORE!

Published by Smartbook Media, Inc.
350 5th Avenue, 59th Floor
New York, NY 10118
Website: www.openlightbox.com

Copyright © 2016 Smartbook Media, Inc.
All rights reserved. No part of this publication may be reproduced, stored in a retrieval system, or transmitted in any form or by any means, electronic, mechanical, photocopying, recording, or otherwise, without the prior written permission of the publisher.

Library of Congress Cataloging-in-Publication Data
Rose, Simon, 1961- author.
  Cygnus the swan / Simon Rose.
    pages cm. -- (The Myth and Science of Astronomy)
  Includes index.
  ISBN 978-1-5105-0014-3 (hard cover : alk. paper) --
  ISBN 978-1-5105-0266-6 (soft cover : alk. paper) --
  ISBN 978-1-5105-0015-0 (multi-user ebook)
  1. Constellations--Juvenile literature. 2. Constellations--Folklore--Juvenile literature. 3. Stars--Folklore--Juvenile literature. 4. Astronomy--history--juvenile literature I. Title.
  QB802.R6574 2016

523.8--dc23
                                2014041041

Printed in Brainerd, Minnesota, United States
1 2 3 4 5 6 7 8 9   19 18 17 16 15

052015
051115

Project Coordinator Aaron Carr
Art Director Terry Paulhus

Note: Constellations shown on pages 6 and 7 are not necessarily in their actual positions in the night sky.

Photo Credits
Every reasonable effort has been made to trace ownership and to obtain permission to reprint copyright material. The publisher would be pleased to have any errors or omissions brought to its attention so that they may be corrected in subsequent printings.

The publisher acknowledges Getty Images as its primary photo supplier for this title.
Page 15, Pickering's Triangle: T.A. Rector/University of Alaska Anchorage, H. Schweiker/WIYN and NOAO/AURA/NSF.

24 Cygnus the Swan